Common Core Lessons & Activities:
Ancient Civilizations

By Carole Marsh

Published by Gallopade International, Inc.

Printed in the U.S.A. (Peachtree City, Georgia)

TABLE OF CONTENTS

G: Includes Graphic Organizer

GO: Graphic Organizer is also available 8½" x 11" online
download at www.gallopade.com/client/go
(numbers above correspond to the graphic organizer numbers online)

MAP ACTIVITY

River Valley Civilizations

Study the map and answer the questions.

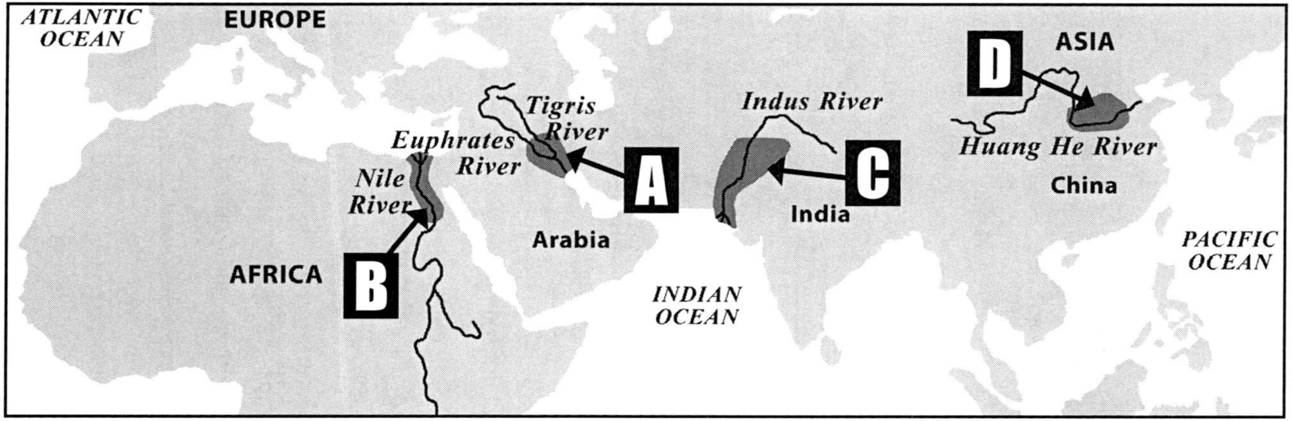

Where did ancient river valley civilizations develop?

A <u>Ancient Mesopotamia</u>: developed near the Tigris and Euphrates Rivers

B <u>Ancient Egypt</u>: developed on the Nile River

C <u>Ancient India</u>: developed on the Indus River

D <u>Ancient China</u>: developed on the Huang He, or Yellow River

River valleys provided a beneficial environment for developing ancient civilizations. The rivers offered a constant source of water for people and crops. The river valleys flooded regularly, replenishing the soil and creating a fertile environment for farming. The rivers also provided transportation, protection from invasions, and access to other natural resources.

PART A: Use the map to determine whether each statement is **true** or **false**.

1. ________ Ancient Mesopotamia developed in Africa.
2. ________ The Indus River flows into the Indian Ocean.
3. ________ Ancient China developed in the Western Hemisphere.
4. ________ All of the ancient river valley civilizations developed in Asia.

PART B: Write the name of the correct civilization in each blank.

5. This civilization developed in southwestern Asia. ________________
6. This civilization developed in the Indian subcontinent. ____________
7. This civilization developed in eastern Asia. _____________________
8. This civilization developed in northern Africa. ___________________

PART C: Complete the activities below.

9. Describe 3-5 ways that living in river valleys benefited ancient civilizations.
10. Use classroom and online resources to research why yearly flooding of the Nile River was beneficial to crop growth. Explain.
11. How did the transportation provided by rivers benefit ancient civilizations? Use online research to support your answer.
12. Create a computer presentation with graphics describing one of the four ancient river valley civilizations. Be sure to explain how the river affected the survival of the civilization. Present your research to the class and discuss.

The Gift of the Nile

Read the text and answer the questions.

The Nile River served as a lifeline for ancient Egyptians. Most of the country of Egypt is desert. The Nile River is the world's longest river. It flows through the desert of Egypt, providing water for people, animals, and crops in an otherwise arid land.

Ancient Egyptians first built small villages along the Nile. These villages relied on the river for water, fishing, and transportation. Each year, the banks of the Nile flooded. The floods brought much destruction to Egyptian homes, but also brought what the ancient Egyptians called "the gift of the Nile." As the floodwater disappeared, small pieces of dirt and plants known as <u>silt</u> remained behind. This <u>fertile</u> soil helped the Egyptians grow healthy crops.

Besides silt, the Nile River gave other gifts to ancient Egypt. The Egyptians dug irrigation systems to direct water from the Nile into farmlands and communities. The Nile River provided a trade route between Lower and Upper Egypt. The river also provided a transportation route for moving building materials throughout ancient Egypt. The Egyptians took the papyrus reed from the river's banks and turned it into paper called "papyrus" for writing and drawing.

The Nile River allowed the people of Egypt to be self-sufficient for food, water, transportation, and more. They did not have to rely on resources from other countries.

1. A. Use a dictionary to define <u>silt</u> as it is used in the text.
   B. Use a dictionary to define <u>fertile</u> as it is used in the text.
2. Summarize the main idea of the text.
3. Describe a positive effect of the Nile River flooding. Describe a negative effect.
4. An ancient Egyptian hymn says, "Hail to thee, O Nile, that springs from out of the earth and comes to give Egypt life!"
   A. What can you infer about Egypt's religious beliefs from this lyric?
   B. List at least 5 ways that the Nile River was a source of life for the Egyptian people.

CLASSIFY INFORMATION

Egyptian Social Structure

Ancient Egyptian society followed a class system. A class system divides people into groups based on their family, wealth, job, etc. Four main social classes made up the Egyptian culture. Each served an important purpose in ancient Egyptian society.

Use online and classroom resources to fill in each Egyptian social class on the social pyramid (starting with the highest class on top). Describe each class and summarize its role in Egyptian society.

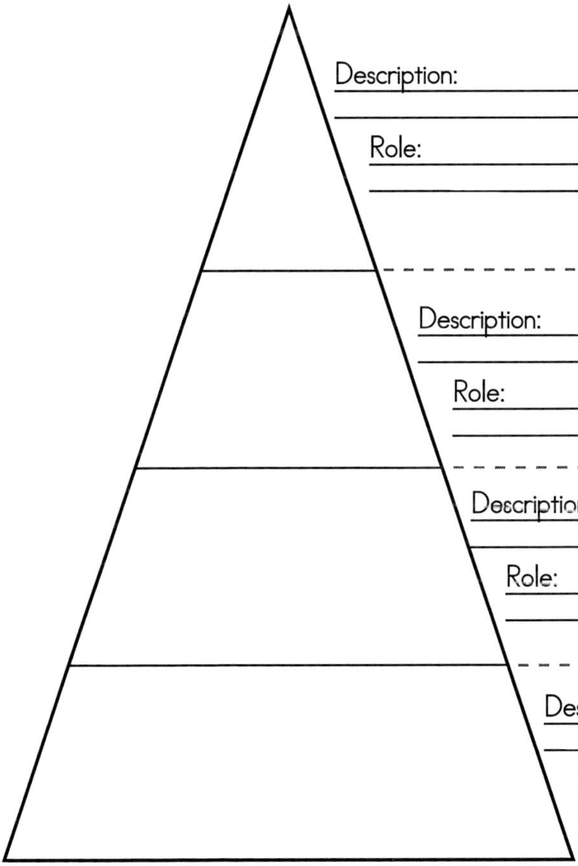

Description: ______________________________

Role: ______________________________

Description: ______________________________

Role: ______________________________

Description: ______________________________

Role: ______________________________

Description: ______________________________

Role: ______________________________

Ancient Mesopotamian Achievements

Read the text and answer the questions.

Ancient Mesopotamians made several important achievements that are still used today. The Mesopotamians used the resources of the world around them to create better ways to live and work. Some of the ancient Mesopotamians' most important achievements were in measurements, writing, and transportation.

In order to create a standard throughout their land, the Mesopotamians devised a system for measurement. They based their measurements on the number 60. Everyone used the same measurements to create consistency. They divided time by 60, including 60 seconds in a minute and 60 minutes in an hour. The Mesopotamians also created a calendar with 360 days in a year.

The Mesopotamians also created the first system of writing called cuneiform. Cuneiform looked like small pictures drawn with cubes, lines, and wedges. Each symbol represented a syllable of their language. Although people no longer use cuneiform, writing is a key part of how people have learned, communicated, and shared ideas throughout history.

One of ancient Mesopotamia's greatest achievements was the invention of the wheel. The wheel allowed carts with large loads to be pulled by animals long distances instead of being carried by people. This improved modes of transportation and made trade with other countries easier, connecting more people and cultures.

1. Use a dictionary to define consistency as it is used in the text. Why is consistency important when measuring?
2. How do you use ancient Mesopotamian measurements in your everyday life?
3. What can you infer about how people kept records before writing?
4. Work with a partner to list 5 examples of how the wheel is used today. Consider objects in your home, toys, machines, and vehicles. Compare your lists with other students and discuss as a class.

PRIMARY SOURCE ANALYSIS

Hammurabi's Code

Hammurabi was a king of ancient Babylon. Under his rule, Babylon grew into a large and thriving nation. Hammurabi created laws to control people in his society. He believed a person's punishment should be equal to his or her crime. His set of laws became known as Hammurabi's Code.

Read the examples from Hammurabi's Code and answer the questions.

Hammurabi's laws were based on the idea that a person's punishment should be equal to his or her crime. Hammurabi's laws helped ancient people live under law and order. Here are some examples of laws in Hammurabi's code:

- *If a man puts out the eye of another man, his eye shall be put out.*
- *If a man knocks out the teeth of another man, his teeth shall be knocked out.*
- *If anyone steals the property of a temple or of the court, he shall be put to death.*
- *If anyone opens his ditches to water his crop, but is careless, and the water floods the field of his neighbor, then he shall pay his neighbor corn for his loss.*
- *If a son says to his adoptive father or mother: "You are not my father, or my mother," his tongue shall be cut off.*
- *If two married persons contract a debt, both are responsible for paying the merchant.*
- *If a son strikes his father, his hands shall be cut off.*

—Hammurabi's Code

1. Hammurabi stated he wanted to "make justice visible in the land, to destroy the wicked person and the evil-doer, that the strong might not injure the weak." How does his code fulfill those goals?

2. Which laws focus on respect for parents? Why do you think that is an important standard of behavior?

3. Use online resources to research the reasons behind Hammurabi's code. In your opinion, were Hammurabi's laws too harsh or unreasonable? Or do you think they were necessary, considering the times in which he lived? Support your opinion with logical reasoning and examples.

India's Caste System

Ancient India was separated into a strict caste system. A caste system divides a society into social classes. Each class served a different role within society. In ancient India, a person's caste was determined by the family they were born into.

Use online or classroom resources to complete the graphic organizer by writing a description of each social class. Then, answer the question below the organizer.

The Hindu Caste System

Brahmin:

Kshatriyas:

Vaisyas:

Sudras:

Dalits: The Untouchables

Compare ancient India's caste system to ancient Egypt's social class system on page 5. How are they alike? How are they different?

PRIMARY SOURCE ANALYSIS

Great Wall of China

Qin Shi Huang, the first emperor of China, ordered that a wall be built to protect the northern border of China from invading enemies. The Great Wall of China was built over 1000 years by slaves, criminals, peasants, and soldiers. It includes more than 7000 watch towers and is over 5000 feet long. Today, much of the Great Wall remains intact.

Study the photograph below and answer the questions.

Courtesy of Wikipedia

1. A. What is the first thing you notice when looking at thc photograph? Why does that catch your eye?
   B. List 3-5 additional observations about the photo.

2. How did the Great Wall help protect China from enemies?

3. What can you infer from the picture about why slaves, criminals, and peasants were forced to build to wall?

4. Historians estimate that as many as 1 million Chinese died building the wall. Considering that information, write a narrative from the perspective of a peasant forced to build the wall. What might his daily existence have been like? What fears might he have had?

Sayings of Confucius

Confucius lived during the Zhou Dynasty of ancient China. He was a philosopher who taught moral guidelines for government and society. He believed rulers should be fair and rule with good moral character. He also believed people should respect their superiors. His ideas became the foundation of Confucianism, which is a cornerstone of traditional Chinese culture.

Complete the graphic organizer by describing the meaning of each saying of Confucius in your own words.

Saying of Confucius	What It Means to Me
"A journey of a thousand miles begins with a single step."	
"Our greatest glory is not in never falling, but in rising every time we fall."	
"The man who moves a mountain begins by carrying away small stones."	
"A gem cannot be polished without friction nor a man without trials."	

1. A. Use a dictionary to define philosopher as it is used in the text.
   B. Use a dictionary to define moral as it is used in the text. What is a moral guideline?
2. Review what you wrote. What can you infer about Confucius' philosophy as a whole from these sayings?
3. Describe a situation from your life to which one of these sayings might be applied.

Civilizations Vocabulary

Use the dictionary and other resources to complete the graphic organizer for each vocabulary word.

archaeology
caste system
city-state
civilization
conquer
culture
dynasty
empire
gods
hieroglyphics
religion
warrior

DEFINITION	FACTS/CHARACTERISTICS
WORD	
EXAMPLES	NON-EXAMPLES

Characteristics of a Civilization

Use online or classroom resources to complete the graphic organizer. Write a description for each of the characteristics listed that made up early civilizations. One example is provided for you.

Agricultural Products and Practices

Early civilizations improved farming practices to meet their needs. They created unique products and foods from their crops.

Economic Systems

Social Structures

Complex Religions

Organized Governments

Technologies

Writing Systems

COMPARE AND CONTRAST

Three Religions

Three of the world's most widely practiced religions—Judaism, Islam, and Christianity—originated in the Middle East. They were developed by cultures that shared a common history. As a result, all three religions belong to the same "family" of religion, and share many similar beliefs, including a belief in only one God (monotheism).

Read the information in the chart and answer the questions.

Beliefs and Customs of Judaism, Islam, and Christianity

	Judaism	Islam	Christianity
Origins	Began about 1800 B.C.E. when God spoke to Abraham	Begun in 7th century C.E. by Muhammad	Christianity began with Jesus in first century C.E.
Beliefs	Believe in Abraham and Moses as prophets	Believe in Abraham and Moses as prophets; Muhammad is last prophet	Believe in Abraham and Moses as prophets
The Messiah	Jews are still awaiting the Messiah	Believe Jesus was a prophet	Believe Jesus is the Son of God, the Messiah
Sacred Book(s)	Old Testament of Bible, the Talmud	Parts of the Bible's Old and New Testaments and the Quran	Old and New Testaments of the Bible
Sacred Places	Remains of the Jerusalem temple, Hebron, Palestine, burial place of Abraham	Holy cities of Mecca and Medina; Jerusalem	Many places in the Holy Land (parts of Israel) where Jesus lived

1. A. List 3 differences between Islam and Christianity.
   B. List 3 differences between Christianity and Judaism.
   C. List 3 differences between Judaism and Islam.
2. List 3-5 common characteristics shared by Judaism, Christianity, and Islam.
3. What inferences can you make about why these religions originated in the Middle East?
4. Research the sacred places of each religion. Explain why each place is sacred.
5. Compare and contrast Christianity, Judaism, and Islam by completing the graphic organizer.

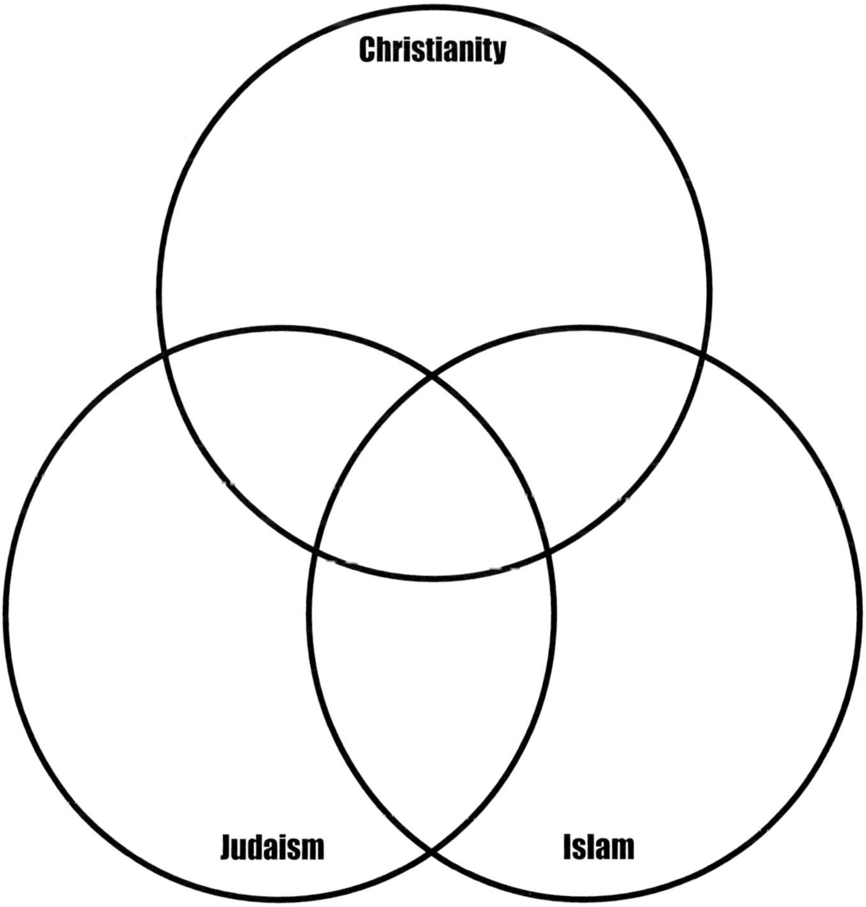

The Incas

Read the text and answer the questions.

The Incas settled along the west coast of South America around 1200 C.E. At the height of its success, the Inca Empire covered modern day Ecuador, Peru, and parts of Bolivia, Argentina, and Chile. The Incas lived in the harsh environment of the Andes Mountains. They were master builders who came up with inventive solutions to help them survive.

The ancient Inca society was very organized. It included roads, walking bridges across rivers, and well-planned cities. The Incas had a strong central government ruled by an emperor called Sapa Inca. Strict laws required citizens to work hard, but ensured every citizen had a home and food.

Many Inca innovations were ahead of their time. One such innovation was terrace farming. The Incas cut stairs into the side of hills to create a flat surface for planting. They developed a method of freezing food in the snow. They also built aqueducts to capture water from rain and snow to irrigate their crops. The aqueducts wound through hills and valleys to bring water from the mountains.

The Spanish conquered the Incas in the 1500s. Today, remains of their cities show their amazing accomplishments. Machu Picchu, one of the most famous sites in South America, is an entire Inca city built high in the Andes Mountains.

1. A. Use a dictionary to define aqueduct as it is used in the text.
   B. Use a dictionary to define irrigate as it is used in the text.
2. Infer how the Incas' strict government laws aided in the success of their empire.
3. Explain how aqueducts solved a problem for the Incas.
4. List some disadvantages of living in mountainous terrain. List some advantages. Consider food, shelter, and protection from enemies.
5. Use online research to create a computer presentation describing the many innovations developed by the Incas. Include graphics.

PROBLEM-SOLUTION

Aztec Floating Gardens

Use the drawing and text to answer the questions.

The ancient Aztecs settled around Lake Texcoco in the Valley of Mexico. The Aztecs' land was wet and marshy. As the Aztec civilization grew, they needed more land to grow food. While they could have expanded to dry land, their crops would not be protected from outside enemies. The Aztecs devised a solution called a "chinampa." This was a floating garden to keep their crops close and protected.

The Aztecs created chinampas by building large, flat rafts and anchoring them to trees or to the bottom of shallow marshland. They piled mud and dying vegetation on top of the rafts, covered them with a layer of soil, and planted seeds. The rafts floated in the lake and marsh areas. Chinampas were very successful and produced large harvests of food for the Aztecs.

1. What caused the Aztecs to invent the chinampa?
2. List 3-5 ways the chinampas provided a solution for the Aztecs.
3. Take on the role of a newspaper reporter in the days of the Aztecs. Use the text and illustration to write an article describing chinampas. Use the five W's of journalism: who, what, when, where, and why. Include fictional quotes from Aztec farmers whom you "interview." Proofread and edit your work.

Montezuma's View

Read the text and answer the questions.

The ancient Aztecs were known as brutal warriors. They conquered lands around them with their powerful armies and took thousands of captives. The Aztecs believed their success was due to favor from their gods.

The Aztec capital city of Tenochtitlan had two large pyramids serving as temples to their war god and rain god. The Aztecs believed they had to offer human sacrifices to please their gods. They offered the hearts of their captives to their gods at the top of the pyramid temples.

The more powerful the Aztec empire became, the more human sacrifices they offered to their gods. When Spanish explorer Hernán Cortés and his men arrived in the early 1500s, the Aztec empire was very powerful. Their cities were organized, their people educated, and their royalty rich. The explorers, however, were shocked by the human sacrifices they saw. Cortés told King Montezuma that gods who demanded human blood must be devils.

Montezuma's Response to Cortés

"If I had known that you would have said such defamatory things I would not have shown you my gods, we consider them to be very good, for they give us health and rains and good seed times and seasons and as many victories as we desire and we are obliged to worship them and make sacrifices, and I pray you not to say another word to their dishonor."

1. Use a dictionary to define defamatory as it is used in the text.
2. Infer how the Aztec's religious beliefs and practices affected their relationship with surrounding tribes.
3. What is the tone of Montezuma's response to Cortés? Why?
4. Do you agree with Herńan Cortés' belief that a god that demands human blood must be a devil? Use logical reasoning for your opinion.

Accomplishments of the Maya

Read the text and answer the questions.

The Ancient Maya settled in Central America near present-day Mexico, Belize, and Guatemala. The Maya were an advanced civilization known for their architecture, astronomy, writing system, and mathematics.

The Maya built organized cities with large palaces as well as pyramids. They had no access to modern metal tools, but still managed to build elaborate, well-designed structures. Their flat-topped pyramids served as temples for the many Maya gods. Each Maya city was organized with a marketplace, plaza, temple, ball court, and palace.

The Maya were also known for their interest in astronomy. They watched the stars closely to keep track of yearly patterns. This helped them know the best times to plant crops and harvest them. The Mayas also studied the movement of stars and planets, which they believed were directly related to their gods. They even built temples at points where certain stars and planets aligned.

The Maya also had an advanced system of hieroglyphics that they used to record their history. The Maya also excelled in mathematics. They used a system of bars and dots to write numbers. They created elaborate calendars, including a solar calendar of 365 days.

1. A. Use a dictionary to define astronomy as it is used in the text.
   B. Use a dictionary to define hieroglyphics as it is used in the text.
2. List 4 main achievements developed by the Maya.
3. Research the term "solar calendar." How does the creation of a solar calendar connect to the Maya interest in astronomy?
4. Divide into groups. Use online research to create a computer presentation highlighting the achievements of the Maya. Be sure to include photographs and graphics. Which Maya achievements have influenced society today? Present your work to the class and discuss.

Maya Beauty Standards

Read the narrative and answer the quetions.

Soon I will be taking some more steps to become a beautiful Maya woman instead of a little girl. It can be a painful process sometimes, but it is worth it! The process began when I was a baby. My mother, like all Maya mothers, bound a flat board to my forehead to make my forehead longer and slant backwards. Once my skull bones hardened, my forehead had the perfect look.

Now that I'm old enough, I will be able to file my teeth! I am thinking of filing the front four teeth to points, and grinding my side teeth so they are shorter than the others. I might even drill some holes in my teeth so I can insert colored stones like jade in them. Oh—did I tell you I am cross-eyed? My mother attached tiny balls to my hair and let them fall on my face between my eyes. When you stare at them long enough, your eyes cross!

I also plan to get my ears, nose, and lips pierced. My mother already has some beautiful jewelry I can't wait to wear on my nose and lips. And speaking of my nose, I wear a special nosepiece to squeeze my nose into just the perfect shape. Of course, I'll be getting several tattoos as well. I want something bright and colorful on both arms that spreads up my neck. But that won't be for a while—after I get married!

1. List 3-5 ways the Maya view of beauty differs from your view of beauty.
2. Describe the tone of this journal entry. Use evidence from the text to support your answer.
3. What inferences can you make about how the idea of beauty is formed? What might make something beautiful to one person and not to another?
4. What is your reaction to the narrative? Describe how you feel when you read it.
5. Write a fictional narrative from the perspective of a young girl in American society today. What types of things will she do to make herself "beautiful"?

MAP AND TEXT ACTIVITY

Ancient Greece Geography

Read the text, study the map, and answer the questions.

Ancient Greece was situated in a mountainous region mostly surrounded by water. As a result, Greek settlements were often isolated from each other. Because of this isolation, individual city-states were formed. A city-state is a city that forms an independent state with the territory around them. City-states were located in valleys between mountains and on coastal plains.

Greek city-states developed their own language, culture, religion, and identity. Athens and Sparta were the two most populated city-states in ancient Greece.

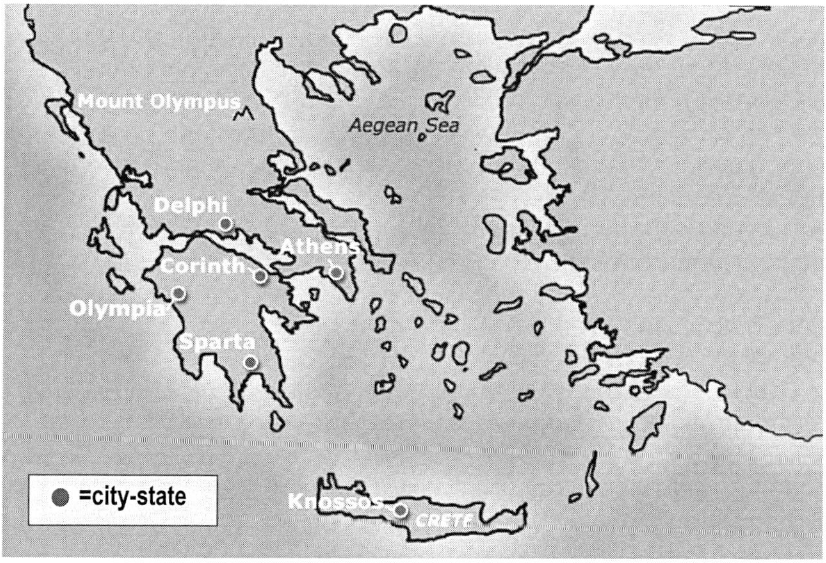

1. A. Identify each city-state labeled on the map. Circle them.
   B. What geographical characteristic can you identify about each city-state?
2. Summarize the main idea of the text.
3. Predict how Greece's settlement may have been different if the terrain was not mountainous.
4. What inferences can you make about why unification was difficult for ancient Greece city-states?

Achievements of Ancient Rome

Read the text and answer the questions.

Ancient Rome grew to be one of the largest and most powerful empires in history. At its height of power in the second century C.E., the Roman Empire spread across Europe, northern Africa, and Asia. The Roman Empire had numerous achievements and an important impact on the Western world.

- **Architecture:** The Romans built many structures, including roads, aqueducts, temples, and amphitheaters. Rome, the capital of the Roman Empire, showcases many achievements of Roman architecture like the Colosseum, a huge outdoor stadium. It is believed that the Romans were the first to use concrete in their construction methods.
- **Army:** The Roman army was expertly organized and powerful. It conquered new lands, held off "barbarian" attacks, and governed distant conquered lands.
- **Language:** Romance languages such as Spanish, French, and Italian came from Latin, the Roman language.
- **Law:** Romans created their own set of laws. Many of their concepts are still used today, like "a person is innocent until proven guilty."
- **Other:** The Romans had many other achievements in areas such as literature, art, government, science, and religion.

1. A. Use a dictionary to define achievement as it is used in the text. List several synonyms.
   B. Use a dictionary to define concrete as it is used in the text.
2. Summarize the main idea of the text.
3. Using online and classroom resources, research and list 3-5 achievements of the Roman Empire not described in the text. Discuss your findings with the class.
4. Infer how the invention of concrete contributed to the design and endurance of Roman architecture. Predict what would have happened to Roman structures without the use of concrete.

Greek and Roman Empires

Use the Venn diagram to compare and contrast the Greek and Roman empires.

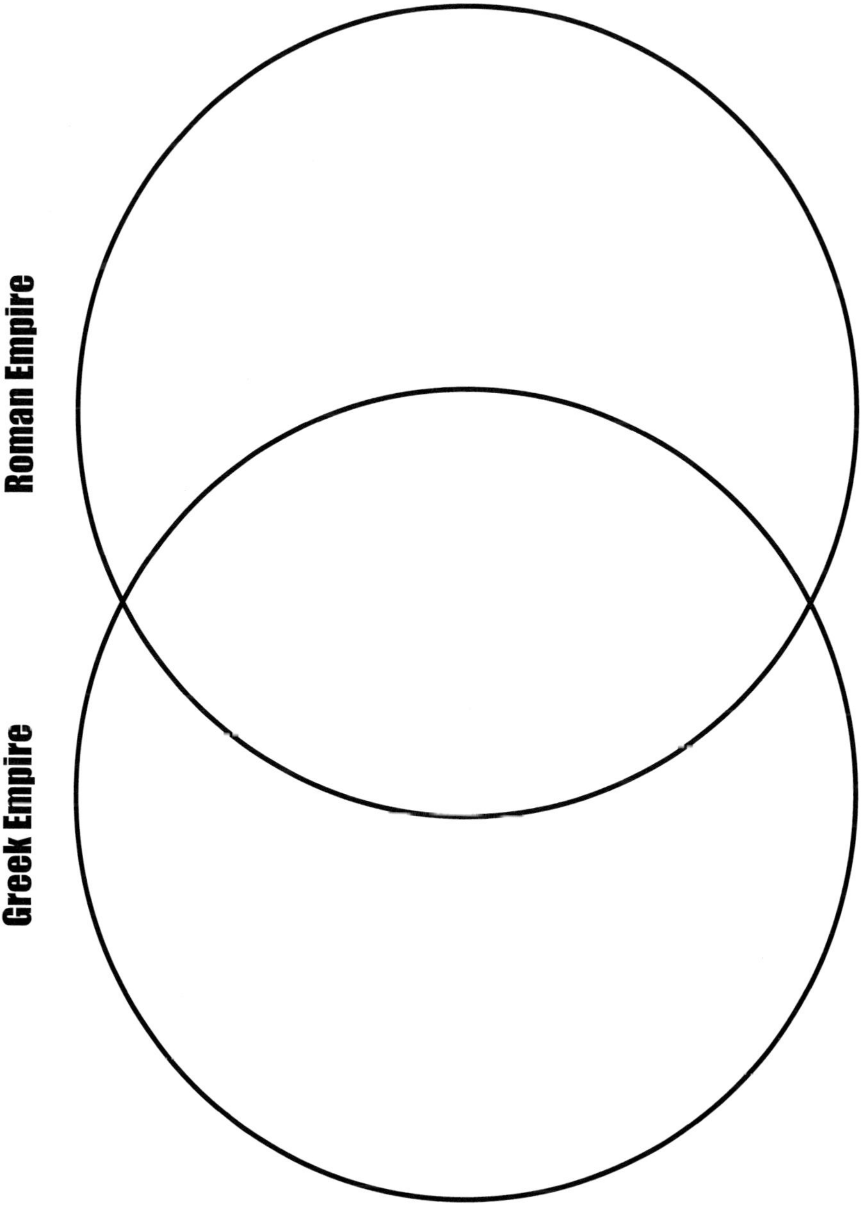

Correlations to Common Core State Standards

For your convenience, correlations are listed page-by-page and for the entire book!

This book is correlated to the Common Core State Standards for English Language Arts grades 3-8, and to Common Core State Standards for Literacy in History, Science, & Technological Subjects grades 6-8.

Correlations are highlighted in gray.

PAGE #	READING *Includes:* RI: Reading Informational Text RH: Reading History	WRITING *Includes:* W: Writing WHST: Writing History, Science, & Technology	LANGUAGE *Includes:* L: Language LF: Language Foundational Skills	SPEAKING & LISTENING *Includes:* SL: Speaking & Listening
2-3	RI RH **1** 2 **3** 4 **5** 6 **7** 8 9 **10**	W WHST 1 **2** 3 **4** 5 **6** **7** 8 **9** **10**	L LF 1 2 3 4 5 **6**	SL **1** **2** 3 **4** **5** **6**
4	RI RH **1** **2** **3** **4** 5 6 7 8 9 **10**	W WHST 1 **2** 3 **4** 5 6 7 8 9 **10**	L LF 1 2 3 **4** **5** **6**	SL 1 2 3 4 5 6
5	RI RH 1 2 **3** **4** 5 6 **7** 8 9 **10**	W WHST 1 **2** 3 **4** 5 6 **7** 8 **9** **10**	L LF 1 2 3 4 5 **6**	SL 1 2 3 4 5 6
6	RI RH **1** 2 **3** **4** 5 6 7 8 9 **10**	W WHST 1 **2** 3 **4** 5 6 **7** **8** 9 **10**	L LF 1 2 3 **4** 5 6	SL **1** 2 3 **4** 5 **6**
7	RI RH **1** 2 **3** 4 **5** **6** **7** **8** **9** **10**	W WHST **1** **2** 3 **4** 5 6 **7** **8** 9 10	L LF 1 2 3 4 **5** **6**	SL 1 2 3 4 5 6
8	RI RH **1** 2 **3** **4** 5 6 **7** 8 9 **10**	W WHST 1 **2** 3 **4** 5 6 **7** 8 9 **10**	L LF 1 2 3 **4** 5 **6**	SL 1 2 3 4 5 6
9	RI RH 1 2 **3** 4 5 **6** **7** 8 9 **10**	W WHST 1 2 **3** **4** 5 6 7 **8** 9 **10**	L LF 1 2 3 4 5 **6**	SL 1 2 3 4 5 6
10	RI RH 1 2 **3** **4** **5** 6 7 8 **9** **10**	W WHST **1** **2** 3 **4** 5 6 7 **8** 9 **10**	L LF 1 2 3 **4** **5** **6**	SL 1 2 3 4 5 6
11	RI RH 1 2 3 **4** 5 6 7 8 9 **10**	W WHST 1 2 3 **4** 5 6 7 8 9 10	L LF 1 2 3 **4** 5 **6**	SL 1 2 3 4 5 6
12-13	RI RH 1 2 **3** 4 5 6 **7** 8 9 **10**	W WHST 1 **2** 3 **4** 5 6 **7** 8 **9** **10**	L LF 1 2 3 **4** 5 **6**	SL 1 2 3 4 5 6
14-15	RI RH **1** 2 3 **4** 5 6 **7** 8 9 **10**	W WHST 1 **2** 3 **4** 5 6 7 8 9 **10**	L LF 1 2 3 **4** 5 **6**	SL 1 2 3 4 5 6
16	RI RH **1** 2 **3** **4** **5** 6 7 8 9 **10**	W WHST 1 **2** 3 **4** 5 **6** **7** 8 9 **10**	L LF 1 2 3 **4** 5 **6**	SL 1 2 3 4 5 6
17	RI RH **1** 2 **3** 4 **5** **6** **7** 8 9 **10**	W WHST 1 **2** **3** **4** **5** 6 7 **8** 9 **10**	L LF 1 2 3 4 5 **6**	SL 1 2 3 4 5 6
18	RI RH **1** 2 **3** **4** 5 **6** 7 8 **9** **10**	W WHST **1** **2** 3 **4** 5 6 7 **8** **9** **10**	L LF 1 2 3 **4** **5** **6**	SL 1 2 3 4 5 6
19	RI RH **1** **2** 3 **4** 5 6 7 8 9 **10**	W WHST 1 **2** 3 **4** 5 **6** **7** 8 **9** **10**	L LF 1 2 3 **4** 5 **6**	SL **1** **2** 3 **4** **5** **6**
20	RI RH **1** **2** 3 4 **5** 6 7 **8** 9 **10**	W WHST 1 **2** **3** **4** 5 6 7 **8** **9** **10**	L LF 1 2 3 4 **5** **6**	SL 1 2 3 4 5 6
21	RI RH **1** **2** 3 4 5 6 **7** 8 9 **10**	W WHST 1 **2** 3 **4** 5 6 7 8 9 **10**	L LF 1 2 3 4 5 6	SL 1 2 3 4 5 6
22	RI RH **1** **2** **3** **4** 5 6 7 8 **9** **10**	W WHST 1 **2** 3 **4** 5 **6** **7** **8** 9 **10**	L LF 1 2 3 **4** 5 6	SL **1** **2** 3 **4** **5** **6**
23	RI RH 1 2 3 4 5 6 **7** 8 **9** 10	W WHST 1 2 3 **4** 5 6 7 8 9 **10**	L LF 1 2 3 4 5 **6**	SL 1 2 3 4 5 6
COMPLETE BOOK	RI RH **1** **2** **3** **4** **5** **6** **7** **8** **9** **10**	W WHST **1** **2** **3** **4** **5** **6** **7** **8** **9** **10**	L LF 1 2 3 **4** **5** **6**	SL **1** **2** 3 **4** **5** **6**

For the complete Common Core standard identifier, combine your grade + "." + letter code above + "." + number code above.

In addition to the correlations indicated here, the activities may be adapted or expanded to align to additional standards and to meet the diverse needs of your unique students!